Lao Tzu's
Memorable Quotes

SAM SAMRETH

Published by Karisma Garden

Contents

01 About Lao Tzu — 1-2

02 Lao Tzu's Memorable Quotes — 3-45

03 The End — 46

04 Thank you — 47

ABOUT

Lao Tzu

571 - 6th BCE

Taoism Philosopher

ABOUT

Name: Lao Tzu

Born: 571 BCE, Chu

Died: 5th Century BC

Lao Tzu or Laozi (老子) is an ancient Chinese philosopher and author of "Tao Te Ching". He is considered as the founder of Taoism. His teaching focused on non-action, non-resistance, and flowing with nature.

QUOTES FOR LIFE

LAO TZU'S MEMORABLE QUOTES

QUOTES FOR LIFE

"Do the difficult things while they are easy and do the great things while they are small."

"A journey of a thousand miles must begin with a single step."

"Great acts are made up of small deeds."

~ Lao Tzu

QUOTES FOR LIFE

"He who knows others is wise; he who knows himself is enlightened."

"Knowing others is intelligence; knowing yourself is true wisdom. Mastering others is strength; mastering yourself is true power."

~ Lao Tzu

QUOTES FOR LIFE

"What is a good man but a bad man's teacher? What is a bad man but a good man's job. If you don't understand this, you will get lost, however intelligent you are. It is the great secret."

"A man with outward courage dares to die; a man with inner courage dares to live."

~ Lao Tzu

QUOTES FOR LIFE

"Life is a series of natural and spontaneous changes. Don't resist them; that only creates sorrow. Let reality be reality. Let things flow naturally forward in whatever way they like."

"The soft overcomes the hard; and the weak the strong."

~ Lao Tzu

QUOTES FOR LIFE

"When people see some things as beautiful, other things become ugly. When people see some things as good, other things become bad."

"Love is of all passions the strongest, for it attacks simultaneously the head, the heart and the senses."

~ Lao Tzu

QUOTES FOR LIFE

"The best fighter is never angry."

"Respond to anger with virtue."

"Who acts in stillness finds stillness in his life."

"When I let go of what I am, I become what I might be."

~ Lao Tzu

QUOTES FOR LIFE

"A skillful soldier is not violent, an able fighter does not rage, a mighty conqueror does not give battle, a great commander is a humble man."

"The flame that burns Twice as bright burns half as long."

"An over sharpened sword cannot last long."

~ Lao Tzu

QUOTES FOR LIFE

"Knowledge is a treasure, but practice is the key to it."

"Great acts are made up of small deeds."

"Act without expectation."

"Knowing how to yield is strength."

~ Lao Tzu

QUOTES FOR LIFE

"The truth is not always beautiful, nor beautiful words the truth."

"Kindness in words creates confidence. Kindness in thinking creates profoundness. Kindness in giving creates love."

~ Lao Tzu

QUOTES FOR LIFE

"If you look to others for fulfillment, you will never truly be fulfilled. If your happiness depends on money, you will never be happy with yourself. Be content with what you have; rejoice in the way things are. When you realize there is nothing lacking, the whole world belongs to you."

~ Lao Tzu

QUOTES FOR LIFE

"Must you value what others value,
avoid what others avoid?
How ridiculous!"

"Care about what other people think and you will always be their prisoner."

~ Lao Tzu

QUOTES FOR LIFE

"Watch your thoughts, they become your words; watch your words, they become your actions; watch your actions, they become your habits; watch your habits, they become your character; watch your character, it becomes your destiny."

~ Lao Tzu

QUOTES FOR LIFE

"If you correct your mind, the rest of your life will fall into place."

"Stop thinking, and end your problems."

"He who conquers others is strong; He who conquers himself is mighty."

~ Lao Tzu

QUOTES FOR LIFE

"Empty your mind of all thoughts. Let your heart be at peace. Watch the turmoil of beings but contemplate their return. Each separate being in the universe returns to the common source. Returning to the source is serenity."

~ Lao Tzu

QUOTES FOR LIFE

"A violent wind does not last for a whole morning; a sudden rain does not last for the whole day."

"If lightning is the anger of the gods, then the gods are concerned mostly about trees."

~ Lao Tzu

QUOTES FOR LIFE

"The softest things in the world overcome the hardest things in the world. Through this I know the advantage of taking no action."

"To a mind that is still the whole universe surrenders. Be still. Stillness reveals the secrets of eternity."

~ Lao Tzu

QUOTES FOR LIFE

"Because he believes in himself, he doesn't try to convince others. Because he is content with himself, he doesn't need others' approval. Because he accepts himself, the whole world accepts him."

"When you accept yourself, the whole world accepts you."

~ Lao Tzu

QUOTES FOR LIFE

"He whose (desires) are few gets them; he whose (desires) are many goes astray."

"There is no disaster greater than not being content; There is no misfortune greater than being covetous."

~ Lao Tzu

QUOTES FOR LIFE

"If you do not change direction, you may end up where you are heading."

"Fill your bowl to the brim and it will spill."

"Keep sharpening your knife and it will blunt."

~ Lao Tzu

QUOTES FOR LIFE

"If a person seems wicked, do not cast him away. Awaken him with your words, elevate him with your deeds, repay his injury with your kindness. Do not cast him away; cast away his wickedness."

"To understand the limitation of things, desire them."

~ Lao Tzu

QUOTES FOR LIFE

"In dwelling, live close to the ground. In thinking, keep to the simple. In conflict, be fair and generous. In governing, don't try to control. In work, do what you enjoy. In family life, be completely present."

~ Lao Tzu

QUOTES FOR LIFE

"Under heaven all can see beauty as beauty only because there is ugliness. All can know good as good only because there is evil."

"He who knows that enough is enough will always have enough."

~ Lao Tzu

QUOTES FOR LIFE

"If you are depressed you are living in the past. If you are anxious you are living in the future. If you are at peace you are living in the present."

"Free from desire, you realize the mystery. Caught in desire, you see only the manifestations."

~ Lao Tzu

QUOTES FOR LIFE

"The past has no power to stop you from being present now. Only your grievance about the past can do that. What is grievance? The baggage of old thought and emotion."

"To be worn out is to be renewed."

~ Lao Tzu

QUOTES FOR LIFE

"New Beginnings are often disguised as painful endings."

"Your own positive future begins in this moment. All you have is right now. Every goal is possible from here."

"Nature does not hurry, yet everything is accomplished."

~ Lao Tzu

QUOTES FOR LIFE

"For all things difficult to acquire, the intelligent man works with perseverance."

"Approach it and there is no beginning; follow it and there is no end. You can't know it, but you can be it, at ease in your own life. Just realize where you come from: this is the essence of wisdom."

~ Lao Tzu

QUOTES FOR LIFE

"Be careful what you water your dreams with. Water them with worry and fear and you will produce weeds that choke the life from your dream. Water them with optimism and solutions and you will cultivate success. Always be on the lookout for ways to turn a problem into an opportunity for success."

~ Lao Tzu

QUOTES FOR LIFE

"If you search everywhere, yet cannot find what you are seeking, it is because what you seek is already in your possession."

"Health is the greatest possession. Contentment is the greatest treasure. Confidence is the greatest friend."

~ Lao Tzu

QUOTES FOR LIFE

"To lead people, walk beside them ... As for the best leaders, the people do not notice their existence. The next best, the people honor and praise. The next, the people fear; and the next, the people hate ... When the best leader's work is done the people say, We did it ourselves!"

~ Lao Tzu

QUOTES FOR LIFE

"The more laws and order are made prominent, the more thieves and robbers there will be."

"The more laws and restrictions there are,
The poorer people become."

"An over sharpened sword cannot last long."

~ Lao Tzu

QUOTES FOR LIFE

"Everything under heaven is a sacred vessel and cannot be controlled. Trying to control leads to ruin. Trying to grasp, we lose. Allow your life to unfold naturally. Know that it too is a vessel of perfection."

"Always be on the lookout for ways to nurture your dream."

~ Lao Tzu

QUOTES
FOR LIFE

"Just as you breathe in and breathe out, there is a time for being ahead and a time for being behind; a time for being in motion and a time for being at rest; a time for being vigorous and a time for being exhausted; a time for being safe and a time for being in danger."

~ Lao Tzu

QUOTES FOR LIFE

"Simplicity, patience, compassion. These three are your greatest treasures. Simple in actions and thoughts, you return to the source of being. Patient with both friends and enemies, you accord with the way things are. Compassionate toward yourself, you reconcile all beings in the world."
~ Lao Tzu

QUOTES FOR LIFE

"When the student is ready the teacher will appear. When the student is truly ready... The teacher will Disappear."

"Giving birth and nourishing, having without possessing, acting with no expectations, leading and not trying to control: this is the supreme virtue."

~ Lao Tzu

QUOTES FOR LIFE

"The flexible are preserved unbroken. The bent become straight. The empty are filled. The exhausted become renewed. The poor are enriched. The rich are confounded. Therefore the sage embraces the one."

"The more you know the less you understand."

~ Lao Tzu

QUOTES FOR LIFE

"Because he doesn't display himself, people can see his light. Because he has nothing to prove, people can trust his words. Because he doesn't know who he is, people recognize themselves in him. Because he has no goal in mind, everything he does succeeds."

~ Lao Tzu

QUOTES FOR LIFE

"Thus, it is said:
The path into light seems dark,
the path forward seems to go back,
the direct path seems long,
true power seems weak...
the greatest love seems indifferent,
the greatest wisdom seems childish."

~ Lao Tzu

QUOTES FOR LIFE

"If you have truly attained wholeness, everything will flock to you."

"To become learned, each day add something. To become enlightened, each day drop something."

"The sage puts herself last and is first."

~ Lao Tzu

"See the world as yourself. Have faith in the way things are. Love the world as yourself, then you can care for all things."

"There is a time to live and a time to die but never to reject the moment."

~ Lao Tzu

QUOTES FOR LIFE

"Whoever relies on the Tao in governing men doesn't try to force issues or defeat enemies by force of arms. For every force there is a counterforce. Violence, even well intentioned, always rebounds upon oneself."

~ Lao Tzu

QUOTES FOR LIFE

"Know the personal, yet keep to the impersonal: accept the world as it is. If you accept the world, the Tao will be luminous inside you and you will return to your primal self. The world is formed from the void, like utensils from a block of wood, yet keeps to the block: thus, she can use all things."

~ Lao Tzu

The End

For more books, please visit us at:
www.karismagarden.com
www.karismagarden.wordpress.com
or search for title/author on
www.amazon.com.

9 798346 951278